winning
bodybuilding

winning
bodybuilding

**Dr. Franco Columbu
with George Fels**

Contemporary Books, Inc.
Chicago

I wish to thank Art Zeller, who supplied most of the photographs in this book. Sincere thanks also to Dr. Anita Columbu, Bob Gardner, Jimmy Caruso, and Albert Busek, whose photographs are included also.

Published by Contemporary Books, Inc.
180 North Michigan Avenue, Chicago, Illinois 60601
Manufactured in the United States of America
Library of Congress Catalog Card Number: 77-81966
International Standard Book Number: 0-8092-8110-4 (cloth)
0-8092-8109-0 (paper)

Published simultaneously in Canada by
Beaverbooks
953 Dillingham Road
Pickering, Ontario L1W 1Z7
Canada

Many thanks to my wife, Anita, for her invaluable assistance and constant support.

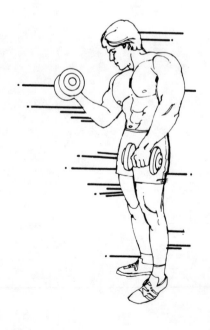

contents

chapter one

winning
bodybuilding

chapter one

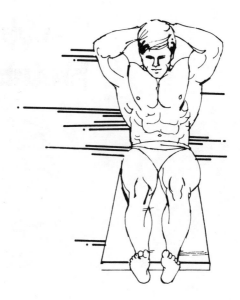

Like virtually every other sport, bodybuilding represents different things to different people.

And a logical first point to establish is that bodybuilding is indeed a sport. After all, we offer both amateur and professional competition, including both novice and senior levels. Bodybuilding is also a superb adjunct to training for other sports; I can pinpoint highly visible athletes from any sport you can name who have benefited enormously from training with weights.

But beyond that, bodybuilding is in many ways the purest sport of all. Long before you achieve the physique contest level—and I want to say more about that—bodybuilding will have provided you with an exhilarating match with nature. It's just you, your attitude, and your body, working together to improve all three. The development of muscle brings with it some of the finest

introduction

side effects on earth. You'll note that as you learn to treat your body with respect, you increase your ability to do the same for other people. Your attitude about yourself will almost certainly change for the better. With no trainers or managers to push you too hard or in the wrong direction, you can achieve just the results you want. You'll look and feel better than you ever have—and remember, what's on the outside of the body reflects what's on the inside. Your circulatory, respiratory, and recuperative powers will all be heightened.

HOW FAR DO YOU WANT TO GO?

The materials I've put together in this book are sufficient to help you attain the contest phase of bodybuilding, should you wish to apply them that way. I recommend that you read the entire book before you begin training, even if you are a beginner; insights and knowledge cannot possibly hurt you. But the point I'd like to emphasize is that I understand that a great many of you will not be interested in that phase of muscle development. You may have a problem with the time required, or you simply may not wish to be built that way.

I am completely sympathetic with that point of view. I have been through bodybuilding's intermediate phases myself, of course, and at that point I took the same pride in looking better in my clothes (and out of them), and my increased power and all-around health, that you will. For me, the real magic of body-building as a sport is that it can be so completely tailored to you, and the precise results that you want. Later on, we'll talk about the correct way to level off your training routine, once you're satisfied with your muscle size.

BUILD YOUR BODY WITH YOUR HEAD

Bodybuilding is far more scientific than you think, and I'm hopeful that this book will simplify that for you. But the first point you have to grasp is that successful bodybuilding goes hand in hand with common sense.

That means training with reasonable—not heroic—amounts of weight. It means proportionate training for all your muscle groups, rather than favoring some at the expense of others. It means intelligent rest and nutrition habits, to complement your training.

Before you put your body to work, put your good sense to work first. Maximum results will follow.

You may have read of such exotic training ploys as "bombing," "triple split training," "super-duper-sets," or whatever. As an Italian, I consider myself a connoisseur when it comes to bologna, and that's exactly what I think of that kind of so-called training. Work *reasonably* with weights, if you want them to work for you.

But let's not forget that I did say "work." My days as a boy in Sardinia efficiently taught me that nothing good ever comes easy.

Building a muscle is no cinch, regardless of how much you'd like to build it. The tools you bring to the gym should include discipline, concentration, determination, and patience.

BODYBUILDING MYTHS—AND WHY THEY'RE ALL MISSES

In one of his charming fables, Aesop created the fox who lamented that the grapes he wanted but could not reach were probably sour anyway. There is nothing to prove that Aesop knew anything about bodybuilding, but the "Sour Grapes" critiques have been accruing to our sport for as long as I can remember. I've heard them all by now, and would like to clarify some of the more common ones for you. None is worth sacrificing one smidgen of your enthusiasm for, none has any merit, and the people who confront you with these misconceptions should be either politely educated or summarily dismissed. (My experience is that the most vocal of bodybuilding's critics are usually built like laboratory flasks.)

"All that muscle will turn to fat." This critique is distinguished by its total divorce from reality. Muscle cannot turn to fat any more than an apple can turn into an orange; they are two completely different things. Sure, total inactivity will cause your muscles to atrophy, and lose tone, size and power, but how many of us are ever confronted with total inactivity?

Long before fat collects on the *outside* of the body, you'll find it building up around the organs first—the liver, kidneys, and heart—where it does its real damage. But muscles do not turn into fat, just as fat cannot be converted directly into muscle. (There'll be more on this in my chapter on Body Types.)

If you're curious as to what really happens when a champion does decide to cut back his contest-preparation routine, it's this: He immediately cuts his diet almost in half. Just about all professional bodybuilders eat four to five well-balanced, correctly spaced meals a day, dinner being the lightest because it's the meal that gets burned up the least. Obviously you can't continue to eat that way in the absence of training, so the bodybuilder resumes a more normal, three-meals-a-day regimen—and *loses* size. That's the exact opposite of the myth! He continues with a moderate weight training program, of course, and while he may not be as massive as he was, he still looks super and stays in great shape.

"Bodybuilders are clumsy, slow, uncoordinated and eventually become muscle-bound." I suppose you could turn up a body-builder here and there who could be described that way; but slow, clumsy, uncoordinated people occur in every walk of life, not just bodybuilding. Meanwhile, my good friend Mike Katz, one of the world's better bodybuilders, has played football for the Oakland Raiders and the New York Jets. Mr. Universe, Lou Ferrigno, out-pointed many fine athletes in a nationally televised agility contest, then signed a contract to play Canadian Football. Former University of Oklahoma and pro running back Joe Don Looney was only a notch or two under national-level physique competition. Cullen Bryant of the Los Angeles Rams and Mercury Morris of the Chargers are just two more pro athletes who are also highly accomplished bodybuilders. The list goes on and on, and extends, as I said, to just about every major sport: Bodybuilding helps.

Note that I did not say that there's no such thing as being muscle-bound. That happens when a bodybuilder trains the wrong way, such as with too much weight, too slowly, overeating, and in the complete absence of any other kind of exercise. Remember, I'm an advocate of *commonsense* bodybuilding, and muscle-bound athletes are hardly an example of common sense. If you have any proficiency in another sport, and you continue that sport in addition to your bodybuilding, you should improve in both sports simultaneously. I was training with weights while I was still amateur lightweight boxing champion of Italy. Today, I enjoy soccer, table tennis, and bicycling, among others, and my unabashed opinion is that I'm excellent in all of them.

"Bodybuilders look grotesque." I doubt that I can change the mind of anybody who really thinks that, but I think it's much more fair to say that bodybuilders are simply not what most people are used to seeing. People of this opinion usually also find something affected about the posing phase, too, but that's nothing more than an athlete demonstrating his personal progress. There's nothing self-conscious about it at all.

For the sake of emphasis, I'll repeat what I said before: I wish every one of you could share the elation that comes with the championship level of our fine sport, but that is just not going to be possible. I can lead you to some very exciting results, still well short of the contest level, if you'll apply yourself diligently. No one will call you any names (certainly not to your face), and you'll be too proud to care if they do. (In and out of the gym, it will serve you well to remember that talking develops no muscles.)

Objections to bodybuilding are usually objections to the muscle size. Following my routines should lead you to increased muscle size plus improved definition and overall proportion; you will reap precisely what you sow. It is entirely possible that you will attain a physical condition and physique that are completely satisfactory to you, and not wish to go past that point. When that occurs, simply decrease the amounts of weight you are using, in favor of slightly lighter weight plus increased repetitions of each exercise. You'll be able to maintain and improve your build without increasing your size. *It is almost impossible to overtrain for definition.* And just in case you do care about what others say, no one ever put the knock on a well-defined build.

WHAT MAKES A MUSCLE GROW?

The motto "Use it or lose it" applies well to muscles and muscle tissue, as well as to less exposed areas of the body. Muscle tissue thrives on activity. What actually takes place during weight training is the *tearing down* of muscle tissue, which isn't nearly as scary as it sounds. Tissue is extremely regenerative, and with proper rest, nutrition, and continued training, it rebuilds itself *stronger than it was before.*

That's why exercised muscles feel sore, or "stiff," after training, especially to beginners. Don't worry; it's normal and the champions feel it too. Your workouts are for naught, in fact, if you *don't* feel this later on. Your body will acclimate itself to your training quickly, and the soreness will lessen to the point where muscles merely feel flushed, warm, and pleasant.

WHAT'S "THE PUMP"?

It's simple to explain, but simply magical to experience. When you exercise a particular muscle, you pump extra blood into it, which helps nourish the tissue immediately. When you're finished, that muscle remains filled with blood, and is measurably larger— and it stays that way for several hours. It's a great change of pace for your circulatory system, and there's no getting around this, it makes you feel high. It is most definitely habit-forming. And unlike most practices of that nature, this one will do you nothing but good.

There is no point to bodybuilding without achieving the pump. Not only does it do wonders for your head, but it's physiologically essential if you're to make good progress. You must be aware of it while you're training and be alert for the point when it begins to decrease. That's the time to quit for the day. Otherwise you'll be overtraining, wasting your time, energy, and enthusiasm. Learn to recognize, too, those days when you don't quite feel up to your usual workout. Knock off; come back the next day and try for your pump then. You'll get it.

No one knows everything there is to know about bodybuilding. I'm still learning myself, and expect to continue building my knowledge of training and good health, as a Doctor of Chiropractic. But I—and bodybuilding—can help you. So can this book. Its purpose is to show you the individual aspects of winning bodybuilding, as well as how to put them all together.

I won't try to describe the excitement and pride that comes with the results of bodybuilding through weight training; I find it difficult to do them justice with words. But when that fantastic glow does come to you, and it surely will, please remember that I told you it would. After all, I'm just supplying knowledge and experience. All the work is going to come from you.

Welcome to bodybuilding. You'll find it to be a sport, hobby and discipline that you can enjoy for decades. Just keep in mind that no one ever started out perfect (or, for that matter, finished that way either). And as the chess champions say, every one of us was a beginner once.

chapter two

BODY TYPES

We have more than 650 separate muscles in our bodies, and there is no more chance that any two of us will have identical sets of muscles than there is that any two of us will have the same number of hairs on our heads.

The beauty of bodybuilding, to me, is that it is so essentially simple: It's your brain and the body you were born with. And since your body isn't quite like anybody else's, it's important to put together a training routine that will do the most for you and you alone. I'm not saying that you should totally ignore what works for other bodybuilders; on the contrary, if you are lucky enough to work out with advanced bodybuilders, you can learn tremendously from them. But before borrowing aspects from

training to suit your needs

their routines, be sure that those exercises will suit your needs as well as they do theirs.

Let's consider the three basic body types, and what bodybuilding fundamentals logically apply to each. The types are *ectomorphic* (slight), *endomorphic* (chubby), and *mesomorphic* (muscular). Traits of these body types may also be combined together, and a person will be a combination of types.

Ectomorphs are thin and linear, with long muscles and, usually, long arms and legs. They generally have their work cut out for them when it comes to gaining weight and size, so their training should be supplemented with a high-protein diet, with natural carbohydrates added. I recommend that bodybuilders of this type train with heavier weights, with more sets and less repetitions. Ectomorphs also have to do extra work on their arms and legs, for maximum proportion; but in return, these bodybuilders often enjoy great definition. If I've described you here, remember that you'll need an extra helping of patience. Your muscles will probably develop somewhat more slowly than other bodybuilders; but they will develop, so stick with it. Also, keep in mind that because your muscles are longer, it's important that you warm up thoroughly before each session.

Endomorphs are the opposite of ectomorphs, so their training and diet must be put together accordingly. Diet is a special problem, because endomorphs generally like to eat; but the right diet for this body type consists of limited natural carbohydrates and fats, and more protein.

Obviously, bodybuilders with this kind of foundation have an uphill climb to achieve definition, or "cuts." The answer is to build a routine of less sets with lighter weights and higher repetitions. Rest between sets should be the absolute minimum (no more than 60 seconds), and more exercises should be done per body part. Ideally, these individuals should set out to reduce fat first, then build muscle. This has advantages far beyond bodybuilding alone; blood pressure comes down, energy is vastly increased because the heart has an easier job to do, and circulation gets a boost, carrying more nourishing blood to the muscles.

While endomorphs would not appear to have the best potential for bodybuilding champion timbre, the truth is that "Trim first, build second" is the very finest way to train, especially for contests. Many top bodybuilders believe the opposite, that you should bulk up first and then reduce. But I believe that that routine attracts fat, which is about as welcome as a shark at a shipwreck. Bodybuilders who bulk up at the outset will lose overall size, skin elasticity, their bodies' natural chemical balances, and generally will collect a spectacular assortment of woes.

Like ectomorphs—but for the opposite reasons—endomorphic bodybuilders need to bring generous portions of determination and discipline to the gym. And they must cut down on their portions of most other things.

So it's the mesomorphs who have the best start for bodybuilding. They're more naturally muscular, with good skeletal structures; but that's a mixed blessing, because they need to regulate their training for both muscle size and definition. They'll respond best to diets that are simply balanced with proteins, fats, and natural carbohydrates (which we'll get into in more detail in the chapter on nutrition). As to training, I suggest heavy weight and medium repetitions for each exercise.

Besides determining your body type, you'll have to discover which of your muscles develop easier than others; you can be sure that some will, and again, this will vary with the individual. But remember that every muscle is a different size. Some will need more sets, heavier weight, and less repetitions; some will need lighter weight and more repetitions. Learning this is a trial-and-error process, of course, but you'll find it quite helpful to note which of your muscles merely become sore during training and which ones actually cause you pain. The difference is quite simple; while this sounds strange to say, muscle soreness is not unpleasant at all. You get accustomed to it quickly during training, and learn to look for it as a sign that your training is really working. Pain, on the other hand, is enjoyed only by a weird few, and is a legitimate and certain signal that something is wrong. You treat pain, once again, with common sense: If something hurts, stop training at once and rest it. Severe pain, or any pain that persists beyond four to six days, is well worth a trip to the doctor.

BONE STRUCTURE

The objectives and problems created by bone structure are as varied as those created by body types. Bone structures are, again, completely individual; and I've always found it interesting that *all* bone structures have imperfections, even those of the champions.

I believe that the secret to overcoming bone structure deficiencies through bodybuilding lies in balancing the body. For example, a man with narrower shoulders and wider hips should concentrate on developing the upper torso—mainly the shoulders and back—and reduce the hips. Squats and leg presses are out, and this man should also steer clear of formal Olympic weightlifting exercises (such as the snatch and the clean-and-jerk).

It's all a matter of *compensating.* Thick-waisted men should make their back (technically, their *latissimus dorsi,* or "lats") wider. Short men should work for more definition. Long-legged and long-armed bodybuilders should put in extra time on those muscle groups for proper torso balance.

Closely related to that strategy is this training secret: Always train the weakest body part first. By doing that, you bring fresh blood, loaded with nutrients, to the muscles that need development most. And you increase your energy for training your more powerful muscles.

You should find your gym manager to be a valuable ally in mapping out training best suited to you. Be objective in determining your strong and weak points, and go from there.

chapter three

HOW TO GET STARTED RIGHT

Bodybuilding can more or less be sorted into five stages, ranging from beginners through champions. We'll talk in more detail about each of these stages throughout the book, but it probably would be helpful to list them here.

1) Beginners. We're talking here about those who have never trained with weights at all. Many beginners are attracted to bodybuilding by its remedial aspects, being tired of either an underweight or overweight condition and the abuse that usually comes with it. That's fine. They've come to the right place, and they've usually got a little extra motivation. They'll notice their first improvements in about six weeks, and can only be considered beginners for a few months after that.

basic bodybuilding
principles

2) Intermediates. Many, many guys are completely happy to achieve this stage and no more; it can go on as long as you want it to, and the benefits will always be there. Intermediate bodybuilders look far better than the average man. In terms of statistics, they maintain a 10- to 12-inch taper between their chest and waist measurements, good healthy 15- to 16-inch arms, and proportionate muscle gains all around.

3) Advanced Intermediates. It sounds like a contradiction in terms, but it really isn't. The bodybuilder who is interested in surpassing the intermediate stage is often interested in going just as far as he can. He's not quite ready for major contests but might well consider his first novice competitions. I think of this stage as "Intermediate-plus-two-inches." That's about the difference in size of all the muscle groups (plus, of course, two inches less in the

waist) between Intermediates and Advanced Intermediates.

4) Advanced. This is the contest level; time to concern yourself with posing (an art and science in itself), contest preparation, and other niceties. We'll get to those.

5) Champion. This is the ultimate physical condition available to you. Although only a handful of bodybuilders get this far, you might as well look at it optimistically and think, "*Somebody* will." It's a matter of seeing a glass that is half-full where others see a glass that is half-empty.

We began by pointing out a similarity between bodybuilding and other sports, and there are other useful parallels. In body-building, as in other sports, very few will ever become champions; and as in other sports, the beginning stages—where the most dramatic changes of all become apparent for the very first time—can be remarkably gratifying. I can assure you that being a body-building champion is intensely exciting, yet I've had few thrills to compare with the feeling I had when I saw my own first improvements and thought, "This is really going to work."

That's an elation that I don't want you to miss (in fact, along with the pump, it's the only kind of high I recommend without reservation). And you'll enjoy it the same way I did, if you'll just follow a sensible beginner's program. First, there are three "Don'ts."

Don't undertake a program aimed at mere physical fitness rather than real muscle-building. (Not that body-building won't keep you fit; it most certainly will. But you're not going to make the same kinds of gains as other bodybuilders, and that is where the principal joy of our sport lies. I'm pretty sure that you'll come to feel that you're working harder than you want to, that there's an easier way to merely stay in shape.)

Don't start out with a program too advanced for you. If you can talk to an accomplished bodybuilder, take his advice, but don't take his routine. First we crawl, then we walk, and all that.

Don't favor certain muscle groups at the expense of others. Bodybuilders, probably through vanity, tend to work harder on their upper bodies than on their legs and abdominals. I've known men who did little besides the bench press and the curl; all they thought they needed were big pectoral muscles and big biceps. Not only did they end up practically void in real power, but they looked ridiculous.

A PROGRAM FOR BEGINNERS

Here's a reasonable beginner's program designed to train your whole body so it can become accustomed to training faster. It has exercises for each body part, or muscle group.

You should be comfortably dressed for your workout. Most of the pictures in this book show me in shorts only, but that's because I want you to see the muscle groups at work. I recommend, though, that you wear a T-shirt or something similarly light while training. It will help you sweat, which is good for you, and at the same time it will help you keep from becoming either overheated or chilled. (By the way, do *not* wear sweat suits or rubber suits while training, in the belief that it will help you lose weight. You will only lose water, not to mention considerable strength.) Bodybuilders often train barefoot or in socks, but shoes will provide better support, especially for leg exercises.

Before beginning your training, you must learn how to breathe correctly. I know you have been breathing just fine all your lives without any help from me, but the fact is that very few people, bodybuilders or not, breathe the way they should. Improper breathing is a common problem among bodybuilders (and not just among beginners, either), and there is just no way to overstress the importance of proper breathing if you're to enjoy the maximum benefits of each workout.

Most people, unfortunately, are shallow breathers. In fact, the lungs welcome all the air your deeper breathing can provide, and at the same time, the deeper breaths do a better job of forcing impurities out of the lungs. Good breathing vastly increases your

27

power for training. It is most important that you inhale through the nose; this helps filter the air delivered to your lungs. While training, inhale as the weight is lowered; exhale through the mouth at the moment of exertion, as the weight is being pushed. And of course you should insist that the room or gym in which you work out be reasonably ventilated.

Begin with this warm-up exercise: Stand straight, reach up high, then bend over and touch the floor, exhaling as you go down, for 10 repetitions. Then do 25 repetitions of an exercise called the Cross Crawl, in which you stand and raise the opposite arm and leg, your knee flexed. This will help to warm up and balance the various muscle groups; it will also quicken your heartbeat, limber you up, and get you in the mood for a good spirited workout. And always remember, at any level of bodybuilding, a sensible warm-up is absolutely critical.

Your first exercise with weights should be a simple press (from floor to shoulder height, hold, then overhead), with extremely light weight, perhaps 25 pounds, for 10 repetitions. It sounds simple, but it actually activates all the muscles in the body.

Now we start assigning exercises to the different parts of the body. The shoulders are an important foundation area, so we'll start there. Then, in order, your routine will work your neck, upper back, chest, thighs, calves, triceps, biceps, forearms, and abdomen. For each exercise, select a weight that you can handle comfortably for 15 repetitions. You should do only one set of each exercise your first week (a set, by the way, is any continuous group of repetitions, or reps); two sets of each during your second and third weeks; three sets during the fourth and fifth; and four sets in the sixth week, by which time you should be seeing your first improvements. Then, or shortly thereafter, you'll be ready to step up your program with two exercises for each of the body parts.

Here's your routine:

(1) Shoulders: standing barbell press. This is the same exercise you just warmed up with. Spread your feet comfortably, and make your grip about as wide as your stance. (See Picture 1.)

Picture 1—Standing Press

(2) Neck and spinal column: side bends, chin tucks, and trunk slumps. For the first exercise, you simply stand erect, your arms hanging naturally, and bend from side to side *from the waist up*. (Don't more your hips.) Repeat 10 times on each side.

For the rocking chin tucks, sit erect. Turn your head as far as possible to the side. Then raise it, and rock it down to touch your chin to your shoulder. Repeat, looking the opposite way. Do this 10 times on each side.

The trunk slump and return are accomplished by sitting in a straight chair and bending forward as though to place your head between your knees. Again, don't move your hips. The movement should begin in your lower back and conclude in your upper body. Repeat 10 times.

(3) Upper back (*latissimus dorsi*): barbell rowing. Using a medium-wide grip, palms down, lean over, let the bar hang, then bring it up to your chest. Lower and repeat. (See Picture 2.)

(4) Chest: bench press. Lie down on a flat bench, use a medium grip, lift the bar out over your chest, lower it all the way down till it touches your chest, then press it straight up and repeat. (See Picture 3.) And don't be bashful about asking somebody to "spot" you—in other words, to stand by in case you have trouble with the bar.

(5) Thighs: squat. Rest the bar squarely on the back of the shoulders, keep your legs no wider apart than your hips, go down straight, and keep your head up. (See Picture 4.) If your thighs and rear are ample, you may want to squat only as far as a normal sitting position, so do this valuable exercise standing at the end of a bench.

(6) Calves: calf raises. Picture 5 will explain the exercise. Make sure that you go all the way down and come all the way up; this one requires the fullest motion you can achieve.

Picture 2—Barbell Rowing

Picture 3—Bench Press

Picture 4—Squat

Picture 5—Calf Raise

(7) Triceps: pushups. Surely you know what these are. After several weeks, try putting your feet on a bench, and moving your hands closer together. Another advanced form of this exercise is to elevate the feet and place the hands on two benches or chairs.

(8) Biceps: dumbbell curl. I'm seated, in Picture 6, because I find it helps limit the movement to my arm, with minimum "cheating," but you may prefer to stand. You grip the dumbbell palm up, bring it up to shoulder height, lower, and repeat. You can exercise your arms one at a time, two at a time, or alternating. Later on, when you add other curling exercises, be sure you begin with dumbbells. They're safer, and even more important, they're more effective.

(9) Forearms: one-arm dumbbell lifts. Grip the dumbbell palm down and lift your wrist as high as you can. Use light dumbbells, and resist the temptation to do this exercise with a barbell, at least as a beginner. (See Picture 7.)

(10) Abdominals: Leg raises. (Pictures 8A and 8B). You're probably already familiar with how to do these. In the leg raises, flex your knees and point your toes, and don't move your hips from the bench. As for sit-ups, I recommend *half*-sit-ups because going all the way back puts too much pressure on the lower back, and makes the stomach muscles longer.

You may also find these generalities helpful:

As soon as you begin training, it's very important to keep an accurate record of your weight and measurements. I also advise taking pictures. Check your statistics every six to eight weeks, and take a new picture or two every eight weeks.

My experience has been that the best time of day for your workouts is some time between three and six in the afternoon. This is six to eight hours after waking up, for most people; the body is more warmed up from normal activity, yet not fatigued.

Picture 6—Dumbbell Wrist Curl

Picture 7—Dumbbell Curl

Picture 8A—Leg Raises

And in the afternoon, the body has usually already taken in two meals.

Keep your body clean during and after training. The physiological benefits of this are too obvious and numerous to mention. It's also a humane thing to do for those around you. And of course you should do your part toward keeping your gym neat and orderly, and insist that others do the same.

Picture 8B—Sit-ups

Beginners are frequently puzzled by all the exotic types of apparatus they see in their gyms, or have read about. Having tried them all myself, even the glamorous multipurpose units now in vogue with pro football teams and other athletes, I'm convinced that no machine compares with pure weight training. Machines usually restrict your movement, rendering the exercise unnatural and inviting injury. In addition, machines furnish mechanical ad-

39

vantage to the lifting of the weight, which defeats your purpose.

"Keep it simple" is a very wise adage when it comes to bodybuilding. After all, the sport begins with nothing more than you and your body, and you could hardly ask for a more simple beginning.

AN INTERMEDIATE PROGRAM FOR EVERYBODY

Here's a perfect example of what I meant when I said bodybuilding represents different things to different people. You can train for size, or power, or definition, or even quickness (and, ideally, for all of those). So you can tailor your weight training not only to fit your body needs, but also the needs of any particular sport that interests you.

Beginners who have been able to put in four sets of each exercise in the preceding section for a few months are ready for this intermediate routine. So are good athletes who may not have much weight-training experience but are in better-than-average shape from their current sports. Whatever your game, this program will give you muscularity along with agility. Bear down here and you'll take on power, speed, and size all at the same time.

The key to this program is high repetitions, 15 to 20 reps for any exercise. It consists of 21 exercises (three for the back, thighs, and abdomen, and two for every other body part) and should be done fast enough that your workout covers no more than 90 minutes. You should be able to go through this routine without fully resting. If you need to pause more than 30 to 45 seconds, it probably means you're working too heavy; scale down the weight until you can do the whole program without stopping.

Do the exercises in the order I suggest; there's a reason for it. Allow yourself at least one day's rest between workouts, and go through this routine three times a week. You can effectively follow this program, unchanged, for six months. By that time, assuming you've kept up with your original sport, you're going to be looking for better competition in it.

Picture 9—Leg Extension

1) *Calves:* standing calf raises. 3 sets, 15-20 reps. (See Picture 5 in the preceding section.)

Seat calf raises. 3 sets, 15-20 reps. If your gym doesn't have the necessary apparatus, double up on your regular calf raises.

2) *Thighs:* squat. 3 sets, 20 reps. (See Picture 4 and instructions in the preceding section.)

Leg extensions. 3 sets, 20 reps. Try to keep your knees locked, as in Picture 9, and try to concentrate on keeping your thigh muscles flexed. (Actually, from a pure body mechanics view, you can only *contract* a muscle; what you can *flex* is a joint such as the knee or elbow. I assume you'll overlook this fine point.)

Picture 10—Leg Curl

Leg curls. 3 sets, 20 reps. You use the same machine you just finished with, but you lie on your stomach. The exercise benefits the rear muscles of the thigh. (See Picture 10 for position.)

3) *Back:* chins. 3 sets, 10 reps. Ten will be plenty for a beginner. Do as many as you can without fighting for them. It's more important to keep the sets close together, with minimum rest. Notice in Picture 11 that I favor a wide grip; you'll probably want a more narrow grip at first.

Barbell rowing. 3 sets, 15-20 reps. See Picture 2 in the preceding section; notice that I keep my trunk parallel to the floor. I also row with a slight rocking motion, so that the lower back muscles get some play.

Picture 11—Wide-grip Chinning

Hyperextension exercises. 2 sets, 15 repetitions. Lie on your stomach across a bench (some gyms have special benches for just this exercise). Have someone hold your feet from behind. Place your hands on the back of your neck and move up and down. This exercise is excellent for balancing and strengthening the low back muscles.

4) *Chest:* bench press. 3 sets, 20 reps. (See Picture 3.) Use a shoulder-width grip.

Picture 12—Dips

Dips. 3 sets, 20 reps. (See Picture 12.) It's important to keep your head up and your chest forward; otherwise this exercise turns out to work your triceps.

5) *Shoulders:* lateral raises. 3 sets, 20 reps. (See Picture 13.) You won't need a whole lot of weight.

Front raises. 3 sets, 20 reps. Do them alternately, as in Picture 14.

Picture 13—Lateral Raises

Picture 14—Front Raises

6) *Biceps:* dumbbell curls, 3 sets, 15 reps. (See Picture 6.) I would recommend doing these seated; that will help confine the action to the muscle you're working. It's important that these be done before the barbell curl, to warm up the elbow without strain.

Barbell curls, 3 sets, 20 reps. Grip the bar at about shoulder width, as in Picture 15. Some slight upper body movement is permissible.

7) *Triceps:* lying triceps extension, 3 sets, 20 reps. Use the barbell, as in Picture 16. Lower it to your forehead, then raise, and *don't* move your elbows.

Bench press, close grip, 3 sets, 20 reps. This is *not* the same exercise we talked about before. Picture 17 shows you that the grip should be no wider than six inches.

Picture 15—Barbell Curl

Picture 16—Lying Triceps Extension

8) *Forearms:* dumbbell wrist curl, 3 sets, 20 reps. Same as in the preceding program.

Barbell wrist curl, 3 sets, 20 reps. If you're really feeling ambitious, or if you'd just like a change from the last exercise, *reverse* your wrists for this one, as in Picture 18.

Picture 17—Close-grip Bench Press

9) *Abdomen:* side bends, 5 sets, 25 reps. A must if you want to keep that flesh off the area above your hips. Be sure to keep the motion above the waist, and feel yourself stretching at the sides.

Leg raises, 5 sets, 25 reps. Keep the knees slightly bent, to keep strain off the lower back.

Sit-ups, 5 sets, 25 reps. Go all the way forward, but only three-quarters the way back. Again, we're protecting the lower back.

You should finish off with any five calisthenic or loosening exercises, using no weight, and about 25 reps for each. They might include the trunk-twister, the squat thrust or "burpee," and others from your gym-class days.

You can complement this routine by eating more often, but less

Picture 18—Reverse Wrist Curl

at each meal. Meat, fish, and fowl are all excellent (more on this in the nutrition chapter). If you're taking vitamins and/or minerals, take them at the end of your meals. And drink lots of water, especially bottled water if you can get it.

chapter four

Welcome to graduate school. This is where serious bodybuilders get down to cases.

Once again, when I refer to serious bodybuilders, I'm not talking only about contest hopefuls. The training programs we're about to discuss can take you that far, if you have the dedication to apply them that way. But contests and the thrill that comes with appearing in them represent just one isolated benefit of bodybuilding. All the benefits that come before that are the ones I want you to have; namely, a stronger, healthier, better-looking body and the pride you take in it.

These are all specialized routines, of course. I don't recommend that you advance to these until you have at least 8 to 10 months' prior bodybuilding experience, with either my beginners' program

introduction to advanced bodybuilding

or a combination of beginners' and intermediate programs.

These are the exercises that will allow you to build all the muscle mass you like, assuming you practice them regularly and consistently. Remember, *proportion* and symmetry are what successful bodybuilding is all about, so be sure to exercise all muscle groups. Too many bodybuilders have pet routines that develop only selected body parts, a practice I have never been able to understand. Can you imagine taking up any other sport on earth and only bothering to learn part of it?

We've already talked about the correct way to level off your training when you've achieved the muscle size you want. Another popular leveling-off technique is to exercise just one muscle group daily. Bodybuilders with limited schedules for working out fall into this practice, too. They enjoy only modest gains, because no single muscle group is being exercised often enough to grow really fast; yet these bodybuilders are no longer in quest of whopping gains. They remain enthusiastic, and still enjoy a regular exercise program, the exhilaration of a spirited if limited workout, and the joy that always comes with giving one's all. And they can maintain their builds easily that way.

HOW OFTEN SHOULD YOU WORK OUT?

Naturally, there are no pat answers. It depends on how much time and drive you have for bodybuilding, as well as on your objectives. Generally, I believe that fewer than three workouts a week represents a waste of your time if you want to see any real improvements.

My customary routine is to train six days a week (occasionally five), two hours a day. People seem surprised to hear that my workouts take that little time daily, but that is enough time to lift 60 tons. In the first place, speed plays a definite role in my training, and that's why I recommend that you strive for as little rest as possible, too. Secondly, I set aside exactly zero time in my workout for talking, loafing, or goofing off. I have many friends training at the same time I do, but they understand that my training is all business. Concentration always pays off in better muscles.

The one indulgence I will permit myself is that if I sense that I'm tired or preoccupied, and the session isn't going as I know it should, I'll knock off and come back the next day, instead of pushing myself into fatigue, boredom, and possible injury. And that's less an indulgence than it is common sense.

So let's say that you have between three and six days a week for your training. Here's how I suggest you group your exercises, in each case.

Six Workouts a Week

This is the schedule I follow. With this kind of program, you'll want to divide up your workouts by body parts per day. For instance, you might train your back, abdomen, and legs on Monday, Wednesday, and Friday; and your chest, arms, abdomen, and shoulders on Tuesday, Thursday, and Saturday. (I give myself one day off for the abdominals, training them five times a week.) A little trial-and-error experimentation will lead you to a grouping and sequence of muscle groups that works best for you. Follow my suggestions as to sets and reps that you find in the individual exercise chapters.

Five Workouts a Week

The most successful five-times-a-week program I know is to train your upper and lower body on alternate days. Ideally, you'd work on your upper body three times and your lower body twice in one week; then, the following week, you do just the opposite, three lower-body workouts and two upper-body workouts. (As an advanced, therefore serious, bodybuilder, you should start thinking about workouts per *month* rather than per week anyway.) This regimen has indisputable results; we can document that muscle groups enjoy near-maximum growth when exercised three times one week and two the next. At five workouts a week, I'm talking about no more than 10 sets per body part, and you should try to spread those 10 sets out over three different exercises.

Four Workouts a Week

This program should be handled in a simple, clean division: two days for your upper body, two for your lower. As with the five-workouts-a-week routine, perform no more than 10 sets per muscle group.

Three Workouts a Week

If this is all the time you can afford, and you're still interested in optimum results, you should count on working your entire body each time. It's not as awesome as it sounds; I'm talking about eight sets, spread over two to three exercises, for each muscle group.

And here are two important tips no matter how many work-outs a week you can manage. First, you should try to add a little weight to each exercise for your Monday routine; that's the best day to train heavy, because you'll have had at least one full day of rest over the weekend. Second, my idea of a productive set in advanced bodybuilding terms is one that includes 8 to 10 reps. The amount of weight should be such that you have to work—but not strain—for your last reps.

Which brings us to the exercises themselves.

chapter five

Bodybuilding competition today is more formidable than ever, and contests are frequently quite close. I'm certain that in my closer wins, it was my chest that gave me the edge, and I point this out for more reasons than my ego.

For one thing, during my intermediate stages of training, my chest was one of my weakest areas. I finally got with it, went to work, and in compensating for my mistakes I made my chest into one of my best features. And one of the reasons I was able to do that is because the chest is very responsive to good thorough training. (The key word here is *thorough*.) A sensible program, followed diligently, will send size, shape, definition, and power surging into your chest, virtually week by week.

And what mistake was I making? The same one that many

the chest

bodybuilders make today: I wasn't building a chest, I was just building pectoral muscles. There's a big difference, and that's why I emphasize *thorough* training. The pecs (technically, *pectoralis major*) are just one of four muscle groups that comprise the chest. Big, swollen pecs that are disproportionate to the rest of the chest are a completely underwhelming thing to see. And to compound the felony, their owners have usually worked for size alone, in the absence of definition or shape, so the pecs are not only too big but too smooth.

None of that for us. Here is the chest routine that I used to make most of my gains. It should lead you to scintillating results, too. It will work *all* your chest muscles and, if you breathe properly, will enlarge your rib cage, too.

Breathing is particularly important when working the chest.

Deep breaths on each movement help to stretch the rib cage and make it bigger. Be sure to inhale through the nose, lift the ribs high, and fully expand the chest on each repetition for maximum stimulation and growth. The general breathing rule to follow is: Exhale at the moment of greatest exertion.

A tip to three-workouts-a-week bodybuilders: If you want to incorporate my chest program into your routine, I'd suggest you do no more than one exercise for each other muscle group, and no more than six sets of that exercise (no more than four sets of that exercise for those just starting to specialize). But whatever the rest of your routine, the following exercise program should be performed first in your workout, three times a week for best results. Go to it. And remember, breathing, form, and concentration are all critical. "Think" the action into your chest on each repetition. You'll be *seeing* it happening soon enough.

BENCH PRESS

Here's the best all-around upper body developer there is. (See Picture 3 in Chapter 2.) This exercise is a great growth stimulator for the chest, and it helps you build tremendous power as well. The correct grip is medium-wide. Inhale deeply as you lower the bar till it touches the highest part of the chest (just above the nipples), then push it back to the starting position while exhaling. I perform eight sets of this super exercise, beginning with a weight I can handle for eight reps and adding weight till my last set is just one rep. But as you ease into this chest program, I want you to begin by doing just four sets of 10, 8, 6, and 4 reps respectively, and add sets and weight gradually. *Common sense and simplicity.* Apply them both to bodybuilding, add some hard work, and you can't go wrong.

INCLINE PRESS

This exercise can be performed with either dumbbells or a barbell; as you can see in Picture 19, I prefer the latter. We do this one to

Picture 19—Incline Bench Press

build slabs of muscle on the upper pecs, to tie in with the deltoids (shoulders). Start with the bar held over the eyes, inhale deeply as you lower it to just below your neck, then exhale as you push the bar back to the starting position. Four sets of eight reps, resting as little as possible between sets. But just three sets for those just getting into this routine.

LYING LATERALS (FLYS)

Flys are great for massing up the pecs. This movement is done in the bent-arm style; a common bodybuilding error is to try this

Picture 20—Lying Laterals (Flys)

exercise with the elbow locked. That's not only risky but limits the amount of weight you can use. My way, you can handle fairly heavy dumbbells. Bend your arms as you lower the dumbbells, as in Picture 20, then return to a straight-arm starting position (Picture 21). Inhale deeply on the way down, exhale on the way up. Get a full stretch on each repetition. Begin with three sets of eight reps; add another set in your second or third week.

Picture 21—Flys (Completed)

DIPS

And now we work the lower, outer sections of the pectorals. Notice in Picture 22 that I keep my head up and the chest forward. If I didn't do that, the exercise would work my triceps more than my chest. As you get stronger, you may want to add weight, either with a waist strap or holding the dumbbell between your

61

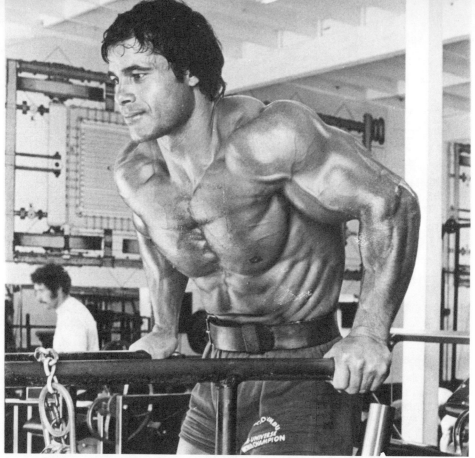

Picture 22—Dips

legs. Again, inhale deeply on the way down, exhale on the way up. Begin with three quick sets of 10 reps, and work your way up to four sets within a few weeks. (These last two exercises can be alternated, working nonstop; it might give you a better pump.)

TWO EXTRAS

There are going to be days when you feel like doing a little more than usual. These two exercises will complement your regular chest program on those days (but should *not* be substituted for any of the above exercises).

Bench Press with Close Grip

This is a good triceps exercise too, and helps the inside section of the pecs as well as the rib cage. Your grip should be no wider than six inches. (See Picture 17.) Lower the weight to the lowest (not the highest) part of the pecs, then press straight up. Use as heavy a weight as you can, for 3 sets of 10 reps.

Pullovers

Here's an exercise that distributes its benefits out over several muscle groups at once. But it really doesn't focus on the chest, and that's why I make it optional. You can do this with a barbell or a dumbbell; it makes no real difference. But if you choose a barbell, grip it no wider than your shoulders. (See Picture 23.) Lower the weight as far as you can, and grip it tightly; the important thing here is to get a good stretch. Three sets of 10 reps will do fine.

You should include some abdominal work after a chest-training session. (I do abdominal exercises on five of the six days I train.) The most successful exercises are the half-sit-ups and leg raises we've talked about before. Do a combination of four sets of 25 reps of sit-ups and the same sets and reps of leg raises. You may alternate the sets if you like.

Picture 23—Pullovers

chapter six

Since the deltoids, the most important muscles of the shoulder region, are heavily involved in your chest work, the shoulders are a logical muscle group to train after the chest.

There's another aspect that the two muscle groups—chest and shoulders—have in common: Many bodybuilders work both groups incorrectly and insufficiently. We've reviewed the pitfall of incomplete chest training already. In the case of the shoulders, bodybuilders forget that the deltoid has three groups, or heads, of muscle fibers, not just one. And all three heads—anterior (front), lateral (side) and posterior (rear)—must be completely developed for maximum shoulder width.

Heavy shoulder work will also pay off in other sports that might interest you. You'll add to your upper body appearance and to your power at the same time. The shoulders tie in with

the shoulders

your chest, arms, and back simultaneously, so well-developed deltoids really go a long way toward enhancing your overall build.

Your basic shoulder structure determines to some extent how wide your shoulders can become. But even if you lack natural clavicle width, you can still have full, thick shoulders, and increase the size of your entire shoulder girdle. It'll take some considerable work, but the fact that you've read this far indicates you're ready for that.

Let's do it.

STANDING BARBELL PRESS

If all bodybuilding were to be compressed into a single exercise, many bodybuilders would vote for this one. It's our first picture in the book, and it's a fine shoulder developer and power builder for the upper body, too. Clean the barbell to the shoulders using a regular grip (about shoulder width). Exhale as you push the weight up overhead, inhaling as you lower the barbell back to the starting position. Continue for eight reps without pausing. Start with a moderate weight and increase the poundage on each set until you are able to get only six reps out of your final set—which should be your third set as you begin this program. Add a fourth when you feel comfortable with it.

SEATED PRESS BEHIND NECK

Here's the best all-around deltoid developer there is. The lateral (side) head of the deltoid gets the most benefit, but all three heads are worked. So is the entire shoulder girdle, and even the trapezius muscles (the ridge of muscle between your shoulders and your neck). Use a medium-wide grip. Sit down, inhale, lower the bar to the base of your neck, then quickly press it overhead while exhaling. Perform your reps without pausing, three sets of eight reps at first, working your way up to four sets. Keep your back straight, preferably braced, for this exercise. (See Picture 24.)

Picture 24—Seated Press Behind Neck

Picture 25—Lateral Raises

LATERAL RAISES

This exercise will add more shape and size to the lateral heads of
the deltoids. Start with the dumbbells in front of you, as in Picture
25, and raise them to ear level. Keep your elbows slightly bent.
Work your way up to four sets of eight reps, resting no more than
45 to 60 seconds between sets.

INCLINE REAR DELTOID RAISES

This will thicken the posterior (rear) head of the deltoids. You
don't absolutely have to use an incline bench, but I think you'll
find it more effective to do so. Lie face down on the bench and

raise the dumbbells upwards as high as possible toward the ears; the bench will help keep your arms in the proper position. Do three quick sets of eight reps, resting as little as possible between sets.

FRONT DUMBBELL RAISES

Picture 26 is self-explanatory. Three sets of eight reps, and *no cheating*. Reduce the amount of weight if you have to, but correct form is critical if you want to thicken those frontal deltoids.

Picture 26—Front Raises

Picture 27—Upright Rowing

UPRIGHT ROWING

Eliminate this one if you already have a prominent trapezius. Overdevelopment will make you look slope-shouldered. Otherwise, this exercise will involve your "traps" as well as the front and side portions of the delts. Use a close grip, as in Picture 27, and pull the bar up above the pecs, with your elbows high. Three sets of 10 reps each.

Generally, the pressing movements are the nucleus of my shoulder program, because they work the entire shoulder structure as well as the deltoids. The lateral movements affect structure less than that, but add size and shape to the deltoids themselves. So each part of the routine has its own role and function.

chapter seven

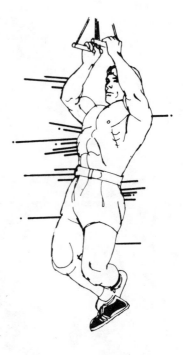

Just as I explained why chest and shoulder training complement one another, and therefore form a logical training sequence, I believe that back exercise enhances the shoulders. That's because the *teres major* muscles of the shoulder help to assist the upper back, and are strongly affected by any exercise that works the upper back.

I'm talking primarily about the "lats," short for *latissimus dorsi*. They're the muscles that give you that manta-ray look from the rear. A wide, sweeping, V-shape taper shows up even when you're fully dressed and contributes greatly to overall body symmetry.

So lat work will widen not only your back, but your shoulders too, if you'll do your back workout immediately following your shoulder routine. Fully pumped lats will keep your shoulders

the back

spread, and you'll really feel and look wide.

My routine will work all sections of the back, with most of the emphasis on the lats for that wider, longer look. And let's not forget that the back muscles, besides being potentially sensational in appearance, are powerful aids to strength and health, too. They're the second largest muscle group of the body (after the legs).

CHIN BEHIND NECK

This is the very best of all lats exercises for widening the back, and it helps widen the shoulder structure, too, to a degree. Use a very wide group (Picture 28). Pull yourself up until the back of your neck touches the bar, then lower yourself down all the way

Picture 28—Chin Behind Neck

for a good, full stretch. I do five sets of 10 repetitions, using no additional weight and very little rest between sets. If you can't do that many reps, determine what amount you can do without "fighting."

CHIN IN FRONT

You may use additional weight (Picture 29) for this version of the

Picture 29—Chin in Front

chin if you're strong enough. You'll find this exercise easier than
the behind-the-neck variety we just completed. If a lifting belt
isn't handy, you can hold a light dumbbell between your legs.
Again, use a very wide grip, and try to pull up as high as possible.
Tense your lats all the way up and down, and be sure to get a
good stretch at the bottom. Do five sets, of the same amount of
reps each time (8 to 10 is ideal), and rest no more than 60 to 90
seconds between sets.

BENT-OVER ROWING

For the maximum stretch, stand on a bench or block, as in Picture 30. Use a wide grip and keep your legs slightly bent. Pull the barbell or stack of plates up until it touches the abdomen, and lower all the way down for a full stretch. Don't tense the arms as you pull up; we want to let your back do the work. Three sets of eight reps at first; add a fourth when you're ready.

Picture 30—Bent-over Rowing

74

Picture 31—Barbell Rowing

END BARBELL ROWING

Again, I'd stand on a block or bench to get that extra stretch (Picture 31). Keep your legs straight this time. Pull the bar up until the plates touch the pecs. Tense your lats and "squeeze" at the top, then lower all the way down. (Another way to do this exercise is to unload one end of a barbell and place the empty end in the corner, then pull up the loaded end, placing one hand in front of the other and switching hand positions on each set.) Three sets of eight reps; four sets later on.

Picture 32—Close-grip Chinning

CLOSE GRIP CHINNING

This one will exercise your full back. It is good for the serratus area (the nifty-looking little muscle group that connects your lats to your ribs) and expanding the rib cage, too. (If your gym doesn't have the apparatus you see in Picture 32, perform the exercise with your hands overlapping on a regular chinning bar.) Pull up all the way, till the hands touch the chest if you can, then let down until the arms are fully extended. Up to four sets, of as many reps as you can manage.

ONE ARM ROW

Actually, I prefer seated pulley rowing to the exercise in Picture 33, but realistically, not many gyms offer that equipment. Hold a dumbbell in one hand, just off the floor, between your legs. Your body should be bent at a right angle to the floor. Pull the dumbbell up till it touches the side of your pectoral, then lower all the way down for that full stretch. Four sets of eight reps with each hand.

Do these last two exercises as rapidly as you can, with as little rest as possible. And all through your back workout, stretch and flex your lats while you rest between sets. Stretching, especially when the back is fully pumped, really helps widen the lats. So does posing. In fact, whether you're interested in bodybuilding contests or not, you'll find posing to be a valuable ally. Not only does it let you check your progress, but it contributes greatly to your definition and separation, too. So overcome your self-consciousness about posing. It'll pay off in more shape and control, not just in the upper back but in all your muscle groups.

Picture 33—One-arm Row

chapter eight

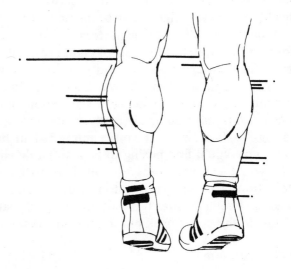

A Harry Belafonte calypso hit years back had as its theme, "House built on a weak foundation cannot stand."

Your legs are not only your bodybuilding foundation, but the foundation of virtually all your strength. (The right way to pick up anything—a barbell, a package, or even a stubborn window— is to let your legs do the work.) I know from my power-lifting experience that weaker legs would have vastly decreased my upper body strength.

And you've already got a better start on training your legs than you think. If you're in generally good health, your legs are remarkably strong right now—even before you ever touch a weight. You automatically exercise your legs all day, walking, running, jumping, squatting, climbing. The legs are composed of the largest muscle group in the body, and they can take more testing and

the legs

training than any other body part. It's just about impossible to overtrain them.

So why is it that athletes in competitive sports—the very group you'd expect to have powerful, durable legs—suffer more leg injuries, especially in the knees, than any other type of injury?

Because, for some puzzling reason, athletes rarely do exercises which isolate the legs for training. They do a lot of running, of course, which is great, but has limited developing capabilities. Running is more of a shaping and conditioning endeavor. I must confess that many bodybuilders dog it when it comes to the legs too, even advanced bodybuilders with terrific upper bodies. Those fellows always look a little like light bulbs to me.

Everybody seems to expect the legs to take care of themselves. They're strong enough to do that, of course, but remember that the key to successful bodybuilding at any level is *proportion*. And you just can't expect your legs to grow proportionately unless you train them as industriously as any other muscle group. Maybe even a little more, because of their great natural strength.

So let's get to it. Remember, these exercises are not as important individually as they are in combination. This is a large muscle group, and that's why leg exercises require proper combining. Form is critical here; the legs must be trained in their natural position for each exercise. And once again, good form requires peak concentration. *Think* the action into the muscle, and that's just where it will go.

Don't swallow any old wives' tales about your calves, either. The calves are of as much concern among intermediate bodybuilders as is body odor in a crowded elevator. They weep and wail and gnash their teeth and write Masters' theses on the stubbornness and complexities of the calves. If only they would invest a fraction of that energy into treating the calf like the simple muscle it is, what a better-calved universe this would be.

Always wear a tight training belt when you train the legs, and be sure you have the weight properly centered.

Picture 33A—The Calves, Fully Pumped

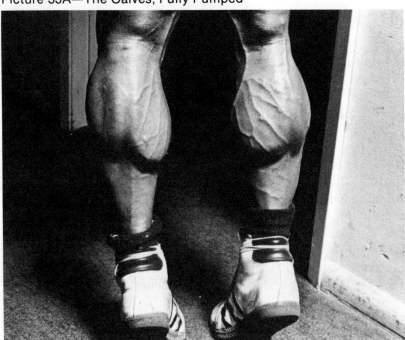

Picture 34—Leg Extension

LEG EXTENSION

No heavy weight needed here. The exercise is done exactly as you see it in Picture 34, bending the legs on the way down but keeping them straight on the way up. *Flex* your thighs at the same time you do the exercise. When you're all the way up, keep your thighs flexed for 2 seconds, then go all the way down again. Two sets of 20 reps should be enough to make your legs "burn" and feel and look great.

LEG CURL

All the exercises in this program are primarily beneficial to the front muscles of the thigh. But those are not the only muscle

Picture 35—Leg Curl

groups in the leg. There are posterior as well as anterior muscles, and it's important that all the leg muscles be trained.

This is the best thigh-bicep exercise there is. You use the same machine you did for the leg extension, only you lie on your stomach. But because all those other exercises affect the anterior portion of the leg, we have to compensate by doing more sets here.

Raise your chest off the bench, but keep your hips on the bench. (See Picture 35.) No cheating here, at the risk of a nasty muscle pull. Put the weight on the ankles, not the calves. Straighten the legs completely on the way down; try to touch your thighs on the way up. Your action must be fluid, without jerking, in order to affect the thigh-bicep.

Do three sets of 13 reps for the first month, then add a set a month till you reach six sets. That's a contest-level routine.

THE SQUAT

We've been over this before; it's the most basic of all thigh exercises. It makes all the thigh muscles work, conditions the entire body, and even helps to expand the rib cage. The thighs, of course, are already your most powerful muscles, so I recommend all the weight you can handle, as long as you do the exercise properly. You can increase the weight for your legs' training for years, virtually without limit.

That proper way of squatting I mentioned is to be certain your legs bend from the front, not with your knees going further apart. (See Picture 4, in Chapter 2.) To make certain of this, stand with your toes between 10 and 14 inches apart, but no more. Place the bar on your shoulders, not your neck. If you hold the bar too high, you'll be placing too much weight on your spine. Use a wide grip, your hands close to the plates. And be sure you look up while squatting, never down at the floor. This will keep you in better balance and your back straighter.

With the bar nice and low on your shoulders, inhale as you begin squatting down. Your rib cage will be expanded when you're at your lowest point, and you'll feel your power. Exhale on the way up. For a good warm-up, do your first set with light weight, 10 to 12 reps. Then do five more sets of 10 reps, and don't be bashful about increasing the amount of weight.

THE FRONT SQUAT

You don't need very heavy weight for this one, but you do need a high board under your ankles for proper balance, as in Picture 36. The exercise will help make anterior thigh muscles long and increase the lower part of the thigh. Place the bar comfortably in front of your neck on the top of your shoulders. Try to keep your back straight; looking above your head will help. Again, it's breathe-in-on-down, out-on-up. Use enough weight that you can just complete 10 reps. Do two sets the first month, three sets thereafter.

Picture 36—Front Squat

THE HACK SQUAT

Notice the pump in the lower thigh from this exercise, in Picture 37. Many gyms are equipped with a hack squat machine, but you can accomplish the same thing by grabbing a barbell behind your legs and using a high board under the ankles. Squat down, but not so low that the weight touches the floor. And when you rise,

Picture 37—Hack Squat

keep the legs bent. (When you straighten your legs, your knees lock, and the legs rest. If we wanted to rest, we'd hardly go to a gym.)

And now, with as little rest as possible, it's on to the beloved calves.

CALF RAISES

This is all it takes: a simple up-and-down-on-the-toes movement that can accommodate lots and lots of weight. A beginner can

Picture 38—Calf Raises

handle 150 lbs. with ease. You'll never get big calves with lighter weight.

Place the high block under the balls of your feet. Stand very straight on the machine, as in Picture 38. I recommend doing this exercise wearing shoes. Most importantly, *go all the way up and all the way down.* Increase the weight constantly. Don't be afraid to get up into the multiple hundreds. I do eight sets of 20 reps, as rapidly as I can, but four such sets are plenty to begin with.

If your gym doesn't have apparatus for this exercise, you can still do what we call "donkey raises." You need somebody willing to sit on your back, a high block under your feet, and a bench on which to place your arms. You're now rainbow-shaped, and you've taken on a rider. Raise and lower as fully as you can, sets and reps the same as for conventional calf raises (if your rider will sit still that long).

After your leg training, and maybe even in between sets during training, you'll find it beneficial to keep flexing the muscles being trained.

chapter nine

I'm sure none of you will need much of a pep talk to get into serious arm training. Everybody wants big arms. The arms have been the most exposed part for just about as long as man has been around.

But that's a partial problem too. Many bodybuilders are not only hung up on big arm measurements, they get completely carried away and want to work little else. I've seen guys deeply into advanced arm routines when the rest of their builds were little better than beginners' level. What madness! It's like trying to play tournament tennis having mastered only one stroke.

And to make sure they've loused up their routine, most of the arms-only bodybuilders (if you can call them bodybuilders) work for size alone, instead of size with peak and definition. You shouldn't do that, because the arm is not like other body parts. It

the arms

has smaller muscles. When you try to bulk it up, you lose definition and density. As a result, the arm *looks* smaller, even though it may in fact be bigger.

The arms, of course, are the key to developing the whole body. So we want to develop the whole arm, concentrating on peak and definition. Size will take care of itself. The program I've developed here is the best of several I've experimented with for the past few years. Try to complete it in 90 minutes. There is no need to change it. The same program can be used for years.

Personally, I prefer not to work other upper-body muscle groups on the days I train my arms, but you can add one complementary group, such as the shoulders, if you prefer. I usually train my arms three times a week, alternating exercises for the biceps and triceps until all the exercises are completed. I train the forearms at the same session, to balance the arms and make them proportionate to the rest of the body, and to help add power to the grip. This, in turn, will enable you to handle heavier weights better.

Here's an important tip: If you want bigger arms, you're going to have to put on some body weight. Remember, arm muscles are smaller to begin with, and cannot extract weight from other body parts. Generally, if you're increasing your arm size in proportion to the rest of your body, your weight should increase 10 to 15 pounds for each inch you gain on your arms. Don't worry about it; that's just the kind of weight you want to gain.

Let's build you a massive, well-defined set of arms. This is as effective an arm routine as you're going to find.

SEATED INCLINE DUMBBELL CURLS

We start with dumbbells rather than barbells because we don't want to lock the elbow joint for our first exercise, before the muscle warms up. That leaves the biceps vulnerable to injury. So start with this, your arms extended and turned slightly outward, then curl the dumbbells to the shoulders together (Picture 39). Lower the dumbbells together, at the same speed with which you raised them. They must not be jerked. Do one set of eight reps, then go straight to the next exercise.

LYING TRICEPS EXTENSION

I'm using the "easy curl" bar in Picture 40, but a standard barbell will work as well. Do this exercise as correctly as possible. Lie down on the bench, point your elbows straight up, lower the bar to your forehead, then press it out for a complete extension. *Don't move your elbows.* Go back to the incline curl and alternate these two exercises for a total of four sets of eight reps of each.

Picture 39—Seated Incline Dumbbell Curls

Picture 40—Lying Triceps Extension

BARBELL CURL

You know this one by now; it's been a staple of both your beginning and intermediate training. I recommend as heavy a weight as possible, for maximum biceps size and power. Start with the arms straight down. Curl the bar while keeping the arms in. Good form is very important, as always, but the upper body may rock very slightly. Remember to squeeze the bar; it will help you eke out an extra rep or two. Do one set of eight reps and follow immediately with the next triceps exercise.

LYING CLOSE-GRIP TRICEPS PRESS

We've covered this exercise, too, in the section on chest training. Your grip should be no wider than six inches. Press the barbell up from the chest until the arms are completely extended. Your elbows should be pointed outward. Do eight nonstop reps. Don't pause at either the top or bottom of your movement. Keep your triceps tensed at all times. Do one set of eight reps and follow immediately with the barbell curl, alternating till you've done four sets of eight reps for each exercise.

PREACHER'S BENCH

The bench helps you peak your biceps correctly in this exercise. (See Picture 41.) Keep the elbow straight and close together, and *make sure you lower the bar all the way down.* Lots of bodybuilders seem afraid to let the bar touch bottom, but that's really the most important part of the exercise. Keep the body still, and force the action into your arms alone. Do a total of four sets of eight reps, alternating with the following triceps exercise. Use enough weight that you can't do more than eight reps.

TRICEPS PUSHDOWNS

Your first set here should employ light enough weight that you can do 15 reps. Then add as much weight as you can for the next

Picture 41—Preacher's Bench

three sets of 10 reps each. Use a close grip, as in Picture 42, and bend forward slightly. Push down till the elbow is completely straight, and do all your reps with one continuous motion. Use enough weight so that you barely do reps 9 and 10.

For the first two months of advanced arm training, stop here. After that, add the next exercises to the routine.

Picture 42—Triceps Pushdowns

CONCENTRATION CURLS

Make this one the last biceps exercise of your routine. Spread your legs and bend your knees, as in Picture 43. Bend forward and rest your free hand on your knee, for some back support. Pick up the dumbbell, keep the arm vertical, and curl as correctly as you can. Three sets of 10 reps is plenty. This is a high-concentration exercise.

TRICEPS DUMBBELL EXTENSION

You may sit or stand for this one, and there's a lying-down version of it, too. Hold the dumbbell straight overhead, then lower it behind the head. Don't move your elbow. Lower as far as possible, for the best stretch you can get. Do 10 reps, and alternate sets with the reverse curl (coming up) till you've done three sets of each.

REVERSE BARBELL CURL

We did, and pictured, this exercise in our intermediate routine. The palms are pointed *down*. Raise the barbell from the thigh to the shoulders. Some cheating is permissible, but don't move the shoulders. Keep the elbows tucked in at the waist, and don't bend your wrists.

THE FOREARMS

This is a tough muscle. It's not as "pumpable" as, say, the biceps or pecs, because it's right under the flesh. So forearm training has to be accomplished with almost no rest. Pause only long enough to shake the hands, then continue exercising. It's the only way to force blood rapidly into the forearm, and that will make the forearm grow.

Picture 43—Concentration Curl

Barbell Wrist Curls

Rest your wrists across the knees. Let the bar roll down to the ends of your bent fingertips. Next, slowly curl the bar up till your entire hand is rolled around it, your wrists still bent. Now—and not before—curl the weight at the wrist. Lower and repeat, for four sets of 12 reps.

Three-part Wrist Moves

With a dumbbell in each hand, place your wrists on your knees (or, even better, on the ends of the arms of a chair). Extend your hands with the palms down for five reps, then, without pausing, face the palms *up* and do five more reps. Three sets altogether, then go right to the next exercise.

Reversed Wrist Curls

Use either the "easy curl" bar or a barbell. The movement is the same as a reverse curl, but move the wrists up and down. Do three sets of 10 reps, using moderate weight.

As you master my complete arms routine, add weight—but don't add exercises. You'll just overtrain, which isn't hard to do to the arms, and wind up decreasing your size.

chapter ten

Bodybuilder or not, no one who's playing the game with a full deck wants a big stomach.

Yet I see the same common mistakes frequently: guys twisting with a barbell behind their necks, or doing side bends with heavy dumbbells. I don't believe in telling the next man what to do (at least, not without being asked first), but what these men have in store is the exact opposite of the desired result. Remember, *weights increase muscle mass.* So your waist should rarely be exercised with weights at all.

The one exception to that instruction comes up when you're doing a modest number of reps, say 25, and you become proficient at that number. You may not feel you're working your abdomen enough. At that point, you could step up the reps—or, you could perform your regular amount with very little weight,

the waist

without increasing your reps, and continue to benefit. When I say "very little weight," I mean no more than a single 10-pound plate.

So the key to the washboard-stomach is really in your head. It's all perseverance. A well-defined waist is exciting to have, but the exercises that get you there are not. Yet they have to be done.

For that reason, among others, I prefer not to do hundreds and hundreds of reps (although many top bodybuilders do, and if you've got the grit, the results are undeniable). I like to do three or four different exercises of about 25 reps each, and I generally go through that routine four times, working quickly, one exercise to the next. That's plenty, since I complete that routine at the end of five workouts a week.

Before we get to the exercises, let's talk about two great waist-training tips for which you don't even need a gym.

VACUUMING THE WAIST

You only need a few minutes a day for this, and you can do it anywhere: on the bus, at your desk, taking a walk. No one even need know what you're doing. You expel all the breath from your body, and I do mean all of it. Now suck your stomach in, without inhaling. Try to make it touch your backbone. Repeat as many times as you can, then relax and breathe normally. Then do it all over again. This innocent little exercise alone can reduce your waistline size. It's amazing.

RUNNING

We've talked about the value of running elsewhere in the book, but it's worth mentioning here because it affects the waist so directly. I'm not talking about jogging. I believe that jogging is beneficial, but the body quickly learns to tolerate its jogger's capabilities, and the only way to increase the benefits is to jog farther and farther. But real running tires out even champion runners. Quite simply, it's really the finest high-repetition exercise in the world. I run two miles on a level grassy surface, trying to complete my run in under seventeen minutes.

As for your training exercises:

Picture 43A—Running

Picture 44—Sit-ups

SIT-UPS

Have the bench slightly raised (the steeper inclines have very li-mited application). Go all the way forward, till your head touches your knees, but go no farther than three-quarters the way back. If you go past the halfway position, you're putting unnecessary pres-sure on your lower back. Twenty-five reps, or more if that's too easy, but be sure to go directly to the next exercise. (See Picture 44.)

Picture 45—Hanging Leg Raises

HANGING LEG RAISES

Grab a chinning bar, straighten the legs as in Picture 45, and move them up and down as fast as you can. Move on when you're tired.

LEG RAISES

I'm doing my own special form of this exercise in Picture 46, but I don't recommend it for you (not now, anyway). I'd rather see you reach way past your head for a good stretching position, lock your knees, point your toes, and raise and lower your legs *without moving your hips*. Do as many reps as you can, then go on to the next exercise.

Picture 46—Leg Raises

Picture 47—Side Leg Raises

SIDE LEG RAISES

Hold on to a vertical bar. Lie on each side in turn, and raise and lower your legs in that position, as in Picture 47. Twenty-five reps, or slightly more.

Do this routine two times through during your first month,

three times through the second month, and four times through thereafter.

chapter eleven

In our preface, we dismissed several hot-air critiques of body-building. At this point, I'd like to take a good honest look at one jibe which does make partial sense to me: "Bodybuilders' muscles are nice to look at, but false in the sense that they do not deliver the strength they suggest."

That is not altogether wrong. Personally, I have always worked to build strength and muscle tissue simultaneously, but that is not the way everybody else trains. And that's why I have repeatedly advised against training for size alone. You simply get a big, bloated muscle that could probably look better and almost certainly could be stronger.

Mere pumped-up tissue will deflate and lose size rapidly if you lay off for a couple of weeks. But muscles you obtain through sensible power training are there to stay.

Only one athlete has ever achieved world-class laurels in both

power lifting

bodybuilding and weightlifting: The great Tommy Kono, still active as a weightlifting coach, won Olympic medals for this country, and Mr. Universe honors as well. That is a colossal accomplishment, because it means that he had to successfully blend two completely diverse forms of training.

My own best totals in what previously were the three Olympic events (the press has been discontinued because it was considered too difficult to judge) come to 930, which would indicate that I'm no slouch. But the training regimen necessary for top-notch Olympic lifting has just never appealed to me as does a bodybuilding routine. It's a matter of different strokes for different folks.

So I've turned to Power Lifting instead. It's a basic power program, consisting of just three exercises, and it's completely compatible with your regular workouts. The exercises are the bench press, squat, and deadlift, and together they attack the largest and most powerful muscles of the body. The bench press works chest, shoulders and triceps; the squat works the hips and thighs; and the deadlift builds the lower back. It's worked for me. I presently hold world Power Lifting records, in my weight class.

BENCH PRESS

You know the value of this upper-body builder by now. When integrating it into your routine for extra power as well as muscularity, you simply apply it somewhat differently. We'll do more sets now, up to eight instead of our regular four or so, with added weight and fewer reps per set. We'll work more slowly, and rest a little more, concentrating on power. Your last sets should incorporate a weight that limits you to one or two reps. As always, begin your chest-training program with the bench press. But at the outset of your Power Lifting, you may wish to sacrifice a set from your other exercises to compensate for the new energy you're now putting to work.

SQUAT

We'll apply this exercise just as we did with the bench press: at its normal point in your routine, but with more sets, more weight, and fewer reps. Again, your last sets should be no more than two reps. Try to go up in weight for single reps, depending on how you feel. And if your gym has a leg-press machine, you can achieve added power by inserting four sets of eight reps with maximum weight. Then continue with the rest of your leg program, compensating at first if you need to.

DEADLIFT

Here's the new one. We'll insert this exercise into our back routine, but we'll do it no more than twice a week, once with moderate weight, once with all the weight you can manage. (And on the latter day, this should be the first exercise you do.)

Picture 48 shows me deadlifting over 700 pounds. I can enthusiastically recommend that you begin with less. But I do want you to build up weight till you can do no more than two reps in your last set, and we never do more than four or five reps with any weight. Work up to eight sets.

Notice that I grip the bar with one hand over, one hand under. The deadlift is as much a test of gripping power as it is a test of lower back power, and that grip keeps the bar from rolling out of my grip. (This exercise will also build you a grip that would make an oyster wince.) You simply grip the bar as it lies on the floor, then stand erect, your arms hanging down.

In any of these exercises, don't be intimidated by the amount of weight you plan to lift. Get a good warm-up; concentrate on what you're doing; and maintain correct lifting form. Then go ahead and lift with full power.

Following power training, I recommend that you reserve two or three minutes for simply hanging from the chinning bar. Most bodybuilders are compressed in the thoracic area, and hanging will help to stretch your spine with your own body weight. Stretching the spine this way is important and very beneficial.

Picture 48—Dead Lift

chapter twelve

No matter how devotedly you exercise your body, your training program is still going to be affected by how you think. It can be affected beneficially or adversely, so attitude is something you're going to have to stay on top of.

The best day to begin your training is today. And probably the worst day to begin, at least from a mental point of view, is tomorrow. I remember a wonderful line from *The Music Man* which says, "Add up enough of those 'tomorrows,' and all you'll have is a lot of empty yesterdays."

Procrastination aside, it's quite possible that you'll have some competition from your conscious self during training. Most bodybuilders do, at one time or another. Your brain is always doing some kind of *thinking,* and that can interfere with the body, which is supposed to be *doing* things.

As you become more and more advanced in your bodybuild-

attitude—the real power in training

ing, therefore adding weight to your routines and working more vigorously, you may find that all kinds of excuses for *not* training are occurring to you. "Do it later." "You're too tired now." "You really don't feel like doing this." "Another day won't make any difference."

And of course, you're going to learn to resist those thoughts. You haven't come this far and worked this hard just so you could talk yourself out of all your good progress. Few phenomena on earth can waste your time and energy as efficiently as negativity can. Don't dwell on the weaknesses you're going to correct; focus instead on the gains you've made in those directions. Use your mind to *visualize* as well as concentrate. See yourself getting better each day. Exercise with full power. Know that with each correct repetition of each exercise, you're that much closer to reaching your goal. Trying to concentrate on more than one thing at a time weakens both your concentration and your body. Remember that no one has a perfect structure, but everyone can definitely improve the structure he has.

(This advice stops short of proposing hard-headedness. If your attitude towards training is just plain stale, and that does happen to plenty of advanced bodybuilders, then you should definitely take a short holiday, say up to a week. Decide in advance how long you're going to take off, and stick to it. By the last day, your point of view should be well-refreshed.)

Another helpful reminder is that you go to the gym to train, not to socialize. I know you see the same faces there all the time. You probably have some good friends training where you go, and I do too. My friends have simply come to learn that I prefer training to talking as long as I'm in the gym, and because they are friends, they have no trouble accepting that.

So resist the temptation to gab, look in the mirror, show off, or waste time. Remember that most of us sleep one-third of our lives; there really *isn't* all that much time. Make the most of what you have.

A lot of the guys in my gym are already working out when I arrive and are still in the gym when I leave. But they're not training any harder; their workouts simply take longer, because of extraneous activity. I believe that a strong body, trained properly, has enough energy to train hard for two hours and no longer. The only secret I can share with you concerning the effectiveness of my training is *concentration*.

You will also find it easy to talk yourself out of a proper workout if you enter the gym with unsolved problems. Either deal with your problems before training, or find the discipline to put them out of your head until you're finished. You just cannot work out well while worrying. Your concentration has been broken, your movements are very likely to be uncommitted ones, and that usually means trouble. At the very least, you'll have an unproductive workout; far worse, you're asking for an injury.

Muscles which you are training benefit from four sources:

(1) The training program;
(2) The blood supply, which carries nutrition to the muscle for growth;

112

(3) The nerve supply, which is needed for enzyme activity, muscle tone, and better control and coordination; and

(4) Concentration.

The first of these is my responsibility, for now, and I've detailed the very finest training program I know for you. The second and third accrue largely as a result of nature. That leaves just the fourth, and it's squarely up to you.

During any specific exercise, you form a direct link between the muscle being worked and your brain. The greater your concentration, the greater the result. It's that simple. Get negative thoughts out of your head, in and out of the gym.

How many months, or years, should you train? The question itself is unhealthy, because it implies an end to training. Make bodybuilding part of your life. You've had a lifetime to develop negative fitness habits; training is going to make up for that. So give it your full physical and mental energy. No one in history ever "got in shape" in a few months. Give your training some time. Put both your body and mind into it, and the training, in turn, will benefit both for you.

Remember, even the world's finest physique first required a head to sit on top of it.

REST

We've already considered that bodybuilding's basic principle deals with the rebuilding of torn-down muscle tissue with nutrition and rest. My chapter on nutrition is coming up. Rest requires no such detail. What's important to remember is that the *quality* of your rest is as critical as the amount. I recommend seven to eight hours of sleep. Some bodybuilders need more than that, others get along fine with less. But however much sleep you need, do your best to afford yourself *deep* sleep and rest. Relax your body and mind, and try to concentrate on your own deep breathing for a while; it's very relaxing in itself. Needless to say, I do not recommend running around well into the night.

chapter thirteen

I can synthesize this chapter for you in eight words: If you're training well, you should eat well.

The benefits of proper diet and nutrition go well beyond body-building, of course. They play a very important role in our general health and well-being. But it was during training that I first became knowledgeable about nutrition. And my years of studying have helped build my knowledge into expertise. There is no doubt that my bodybuilding gains would have been considerably limited were it not for my excellent background in nutrition.

I was fortunate enough to bring far-better-than-average power to my training, even as a beginner. And I'm quite certain that one of the reasons for my early strength was that for the first 19 years of my life, I had only natural food. On the island of Sardinia, where I was born and lived, we had no processed or refined food

nutrition

whatsoever. I come from the island's mountainous interior, where the people exist solely from the land and their animals. The old people of Sardinia live at home, strong, healthy and active all their lives, and that's no coincidence. I firmly believe that the correct diet over a lifetime can increase that life span by 10 to 15 years.

Today, I always try to eat fresh natural foods, as close as possible to the diet which I had in Sardinia. Whatever your diet, you should keep it simple and as natural as you can. And to complement your bodybuilding more fully, you should try to eat three or four small meals instead of one or two large ones. Let your appetite dictate your eating times, and don't force yourself to eat. Your training should help your appetite along, even if you've never been a great eater.

Here's a sample of the diet that's helped me to the results I've achieved:

Breakfast

3 fresh eggs (my cooking preference is over-easy)
1 fresh fruit in season, or
A large glass of fresh-squeezed orange juice
A small dish of homemade plain yogurt (made with raw milk), with Granola cereal
A glass of mineral water, with vitamin and mineral supplements

Lunch

A large fresh vegetable salad, with a small amount of oil-and-vinegar dressing
1 cooked fresh vegetable (never frozen or canned)
A large portion of fresh broiled protein, such as fish, chicken, prime cuts of beef, lamb, or liver
A small glass of wine or a large glass of mineral water

Mid-afternoon

A plate of selected imported cheeses, with fresh fruit in season (usually pears)

Dinner

Similar to lunch. I do try to have an early dinner.

Later in the evening

A small dish of fresh yogurt. Homemade yogurt is super for both the digestion and elimination processes.

Throughout the day, I always try to have eight to ten glasses of mineral or bottled water.

You can see that I believe in food in its natural form. I do *not* believe in protein powder, because it usually has a high carbohydrate and sugar content. Also, it is frequently not digested and/or assimilated by the body. In that case, the user feels bloated, and his stomach looks thick.

Difficulty in gaining weight is a very common problem among bodybuilders. The diet I've recommended here should help. Additionally, people who have trouble putting on weight often have a higher metabolic rate, and therefore should learn more about the art of relaxation. They may also add the following foods to their diet: whole-grain bread, baked potatoes (which are rich in minerals), natural brown rice, all fresh-cooked vegetables (they're higher in carbohydrates), snacks of raw nuts and seeds, dried fruit (preferably the kind with no sulphur added), and kefir (similar to homemade yogurt).

It is quite possible to overdo your intake of vitamin, mineral, and protein supplements. As I mentioned, the body will not assimilate more than it needs. So I don't believe in mixing several types of protein at one meal, or taking an overabundance of vitamin and mineral supplements. Vitamins should be balanced, and taking too much of one substance can cause a deficiency in another. This is particularly true with the B-complex supplements. The B-complex should be taken together, and the different B vitamins should not be isolated.

But vitamins and minerals are both valuable tools. Vitamins are organic food substances and are absolutely necessary for proper growth and maintenance of health. They retain their original form in the body and are built into the body structure, where they become important parts of the machinery of all cells.

Minerals are important factors in maintaining proper physiological conditions and processes, such as the acid-base balance, osmotic action, elasticity, and muscle tissues. Vitamins cannot do their work unless minerals are present. So I do want you to take vitamin and mineral supplements, but I want you to take them the correct way.

Never eat a heavy meal before training in the belief that you're going to work it off right away. This gets us back to our good friend common sense, but there's a biological reason for it too: You need blood in your stomach to aid digestion. If you try to pump that blood into muscles, you can't digest your meal properly. (Or, you won't be able to get your pump. Neither effect is anything you want.)

Your body must be chemically balanced, and so your diet must be balanced, too. That means you need the proper amounts of protein, natural carbohydrates, and small amounts of fats and vitamins and minerals. Naturally, I avoid large quantities of fat in the food, and so should you, but *some* fat is useful. It provides a reserve supply of stored body fuel, and helps maintain body heat and temperature; and it is important for normal tissue function.

Stay away from refined sugar. Sugar is my idea of slow poison. That's why I'm so down on processed foods; sugar is frequently hidden in them without our knowing it. If we poured sugar down the gas tanks of our cars the way we pour it down our systems, we could shut down Detroit. Not only does sugar provide absolutely zero benefits, but it has actually been shown to *weaken* muscles! (I want you to remember this, the next time you feel the urge to down something sweet just before a workout.) Sugar also raises the blood-sugar level temporarily, then lowers it drastically shortly thereafter. Athletes are frequently of the opinion that honey is an ideal quick-energy pick-me-up, but honey is vastly overrated. It is really not much more beneficial than sugar. (My own preference in this area is unsweetened grape juice.)

Training alone is not going to get you what you want. Neither is proper nutrition. It's the combination of the two that will build you a better body. People who are kind enough to ask me how I maintain my definition always seem surprised by the answer: *activity*. That's all it takes when you eat sensibly.

There isn't a drug on earth that I can recommend for building muscle, not even the steroids that you've probably read about. The 1976 edition of *The Physician's Desk Reference* states clearly that anabolic steroid drugs "do not enhance athletic ability." Stay away from them. The name itself seems to say, "Steer clear." All other drugs—uppers, downers, thyroid, male hormones, whatever—have been proven to be totally useless in winning bodybuilding. (There is what psychologists call the "placebo effect," which simply means that the drug-taker trains harder because he *believes* the drug has made him stronger. But that's simply testimony to the effectiveness of the mind when it comes to building muscle and power. The drugs themselves won't have any effects for weeks, and they will be negative effects in the bargain.)

When you indulge yourself in any type of drug, you're risking side effects and your own good health. So be proud of your head as well as your body, and take good care of both. A good body is worthless without a good brain to control it. The best and only way to turn yourself on is through proper nutrition and vigorous exercise. Knock off the drugs and all the other outside stimulants. You'll be amazed at how great you feel and how much clearer your mind and powers of concentration will be.

chapter fourteen

Training injuries, of course, are hardly exclusive to bodybuilding. They occur in all sports, and frequently for the same reasons: Someone didn't warm up properly, or overexerted, or broke from routine unwisely. Bodybuilding does have some do's and don'ts of its own, though, and we'll take a closer look at those as well.

WARM UP CORRECTLY

The world's finest automobiles benefit from a brief warm-up before being asked to work, and their bodies are built far more solidly than any of ours. So a thorough, sensible, efficient warm-up is a must before working out.

Your body has it all over the automobile when it comes to

injuries

warming up. It can tell you things no car ever could. Like just how warm or cold it feels. And how stiff or limber. And, most importantly, when it's been sufficiently warmed up for peak performance. No question about that; a good warm-up always feels great both in your body and in your head. You'll focus better on your training routine, too.

I'm a devout believer in running, not just as a warm-up but as an actual supplement to my weight training. As a bodybuilder, you've already got the finest running tools: stamina, discipline, and tougher, stronger legs. How far should you run for a good warm-up? Nothing could be simpler. Just let your body tell you. You'll know when you've reached the point where further running will borrow on the energy you need for training. Running will also do wonders for your definition, and can out-trim any calisthenic exercise on earth when it comes to stubborn fleshy areas.

Your warm-up should also include a few gymnastic movements, without weights. I outlined one such exercise in Chapter 2. One of my regular warm-up exercises is to lie on the floor and raise the opposite arm and leg (right leg and left arm, then vice versa). I do about 25 reps of this exercise.

But whatever your preference, remember to do something light before you do anything heavy. And if you must include weights as part of your warm-ups, make them dumbbell weights.

AVOID OVEREXERTION

Team sports injuries often occur late in the game. Many skiing injuries take place on the last slope. And the same is true in bodybuilding: *Don't push when you're tired.*

Again, your body will be all too happy to tell you when it's had enough. It makes no sense to force yourself through a heavy workout when you're tired. Not only would you be foolishly risking injury, but you'd make very little progress as a result of that workout. It's a much better idea to take a light workout, go home, and rest. The next day, refreshed, you can resume your regular training routine, and you'll feel lots more comfortable with it.

STICK TO YOUR ROUTINE

I doubt that any group of athletes in the universe can match bodybuilders when it comes to demonstrating discipline and perseverance. At the same time we train our bodies so rigorously, we have to train our minds to focus on our routines . . . *and stick to them.* Except, of course, when you feel tired.

It's important to train each part of the body in logical order. Many bodybuilders believe strongly in doing alternate sets of exercises for muscle groups that complement one another, such as biceps and triceps. That is one of the few examples of alternating exercises I use myself, but I do believe in grouping exercises for different body parts in an order that lets them benefit from each other's training, such as chest followed by shoulders.

Always pay attention, too, to the way you're working the various pieces of equipment into your routine. For instance, one habit I'd like to see a lot of bodybuilders break is beginning their workouts with barbell curls. That particular exercise certainly has its place, but is not a good warming-up or beginning exercise because it locks the elbow joint, leaving the biceps vulnerable to injury.

CONCENTRATE! CONCENTRATE! CONCENTRATE!

You probably take my drift by now: concentrate. Bodybuilding is most definitely a mental as well as physical achievement.

Your concentration should begin as soon as you arrive at the gym. Magical things happen when you focus complete concentration into your workout. Adrenaline flows luxuriously. Each individual repetition of each exercise you perform is done more strictly, therefore more beneficially. Good form helps guard further against injury in itself. And just as you "think" the action of the exercise into the muscle involved, and visualize that muscle becoming bigger and stronger, that's just what happens.

You're unquestionably more prone to injury when your concentration lapses. So keep your mind on your equipment and your body. Tune out the chatterers and mirror-gazers. They're already wasting their time; don't let them waste yours.

MAINTAIN A HEALTHFUL DIET

We've talked about this in the nutrition chapter, but diet and injuries have a closer correlation than you might think. Muscle spasms and muscle cramps, common problems, are usually traced to nutritional imbalances. Heavy training itself excretes nutrients

123

from the body. Many bodybuilders follow a high-protein diet and, therefore, don't get enough vitamins and minerals, particularly vitamin C and calcium. And the bodybuilders who have discovered steroid drugs aren't doing themselves any favors; they can expect vitamin deficiencies, irreversible body damage, and family miseries.

WHAT TO DO

The most common bodybuilding injuries are tendon tears or snaps, cramps, strains, sprains, and hernias. The same advice applies to all of them: Stop training immediately. Try to determine the severity of the injury. Ice applications (that is, an ice cube placed directly over the area of pain) will help reduce any swelling and inflammation. And most of all, *see a doctor*. Don't attempt to diagnose yourself, and don't listen to anyone else in the gym (unless you're fortunate enough to work out in the company of doctors). Get professional help for all injuries regardless of how minor they might seem. It will save you from more serious problems and a lot of grief.

chapter fifteen

As I've said throughout the book, I understand that the majority of you are interested in *non*competitive bodybuilding, and I respect that. Contests represent just one more benefit from our sport, although an awfully exciting one, and by now you should be well on your way to the important rewards.

Nevertheless, since we're all friends now, I'm going to suggest something to those of you who may have already enjoyed great gains and the pride that comes with them: You might consider competing in a contest, even if it's just at the "novice" level at your local YMCA. If you're anything like I am, it's the little adventures that make life fun; the big ones seem to come too far apart.

And the truth is, you'll have the time of your life. (If, by the way, you're deeply interested in contests, that doesn't make you a bad guy either; please read right along.) Bodybuilding contest audiences are among the most receptive and enthusiastic—yet well-

competition

mannered—that I have ever seen in sports. They *want* you to do well. Like the fans of any other sport, they are always interested in discovering exciting newcomers. And whether it's for winning or just for trying, they will applaud you. That alone seems to me to make contests worth considering.

(I've already told you that I'm a connoisseur of bologna; I know a thing or two about ham, too.)

In any case, it can't hurt you to know the right way to prepare for competitive bodybuilding. You might even find a tip or two that will enhance your training.

RUNNING

Those of you who enjoy seeing a .350 hitter take a third strike, or a pro golfer shanking one, will be happy to know that some of the world's premier bodybuilders, including this one, have carried an excess layer of fat around their middles.

We experimented with and swapped diets as though they were baseball trading cards. We did sit-ups till they closed the gym on us. And in the morning, there it would be again, sticking to us like Poe's raven.

Until we learned to run it off.

Running has become an integral part of championship training. Many of us run two miles or more daily, but just about all of us prepare for a contest by running. We all have size; it will take definition to win a contest. And that's why we run: for added definition and muscularity.

So should you. You'll get almost immediate benefits, and a trimming effect on your waist, hips, and small of the back. Running delivers more oxygen to all parts of the body, and its action works the trunk muscles as no exercises can.

Running is one of our special contest-winning secrets. It improves the shape of the legs: The calves look hard and dense, thighs express their natural lines with deep indentations. And of course, those of you who follow the aerobics theory of physical fitness know that running is the quickest way to earn your weekly points. We estimate that a hard-working competitive bodybuilder who combines running and training earns more than 100 points a week!

POSING

Posing is not only the process by which physique contests are run, but it should be part of your contest preparation. Posing is good for you. Besides showing you how you're doing, it helps with your definition and separation, too. Some of you will recognize that posing is really a form of isometric exercise; and whether for contest purposes or not, a posing routine makes for a *great* little two-minute workout.

You'll need an average of 15 good poses for a contest. There's some showmanship involved, of course. The usual practice is to begin with your second-best pose for a fast, good first impression. You finish with your best, for obvious reasons. Your poses must be smooth and fluid, the same length of time for each, and naturally you select poses that spotlight your best features. Be patient in learning how to pose; it's no snap. Good posers always have hours of practicing in their background.

The most important posing secret I know is *always strive to look relaxed*. Tensing your muscles without tensing your facial muscles will probably be a little tricky at first—it's much like rubbing your head while patting your belly. But you can master it, and the added appeal of an unstrained facial expression to complement your posing could give you an edge in competition.

A good tan helps, too. Those are bright lights above a contest stage, and they can easily "wash out" the details of the definition you've worked so hard to achieve. As you no doubt know, the correct way to tan is gradually. In California, of course, we're spoiled in that we can take the sun the year around. We also enjoy training outdoors, and I personally find that the sun adds to my strength. (But I *never* use sun lamps, and neither should you, especially in the area of the eyes.)

If your contest permits the use of oil, and not all contests do, be sure to use a small amount. Too much oil will flatten your body out under the posing lights, and the combination of oil and perspiration is sure to make you look greasy.

Here's a pose-by-pose routine which works well for me. Your own best routine will probably occur to you as a result of experimenting, but this sequence should show all your muscle groups to good advantage.

Picture 49—After taking your place on stage, stand still in a normal position for a few seconds, then go to this "front lat spray" and flex as best you can.

Picture 50—Raise your arms in back of your head and flex your abdominals. This is the most attractive way to show them.

Picture 51—Then drop down and do a double front biceps.

Picture 52—Do a straight left turn and do double biceps from the back, in the same position.

Picture 53—Stand up and do this "side post."

Picture 49—Front Lat Spray

Picture 50—Abdominals Pose

Picture 51—Double Front Biceps

132

Picture 52—Double Biceps From Back

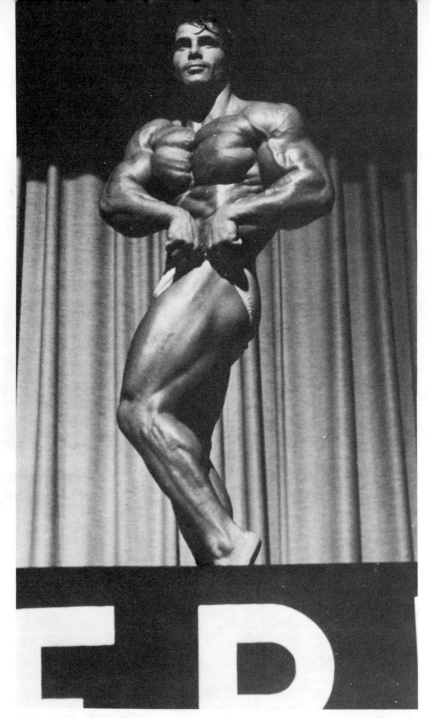

Picture 53—Side Post

Picture 54—Turn to the front and do a front pose.

Picture 55—Then turn to the side and do a side/back shot.

Picture 56—Continue with the second side/back pose.

Picture 57—Another half-turn to the back, for another double biceps.

Picture 58—Continue with lat spray.

Picture 59—Then do a half-turn to the left and show this side chest shot.

Picture 60—Then do a half-turn to the front, for another front pose.

Picture 61—Raise your arms and do a double biceps pose.

Picture 62—Drop your arms again and do an entire front pose.

Picture 63—Hit your last, best front pose. This one is called "Most Muscular."

TRAINING

You must decrease training sharply in the last seven days before the contest. If the competition is on Saturday, for instance, you'd ideally take a medium workout on Monday and Tuesday, a light one on Wednesday, running only on Thursday, and rest on Friday and Saturday till contest time. You do this to increase your body's resistance and recuperate your energy so you'll be at your peak to achieve your pump on Saturday.

DIET

Chances are you're already eating properly if you're preparing for a contest, and all you really have to do now is be consistent. Always eat on time, and space your meals according to schedule and keep them that way. Many bodybuilders go on a low-carbohydrates diet consisting of meat and water, but I believe that is a mistake. Protein is good for the body, but the brain needs carbohydrates. Salads, vegetables, fruits, yogurt all offer a

Picture 54—Front Pose

Picture 55—Side/Back Shot

Picture 56—Second Side/Back Pose

Picture 57—Double Biceps From Back

139

Picture 58—Lat Spray

Picture 59—Side Chest Shot

Picture 60—Another Front Pose

Picture 61—Double Biceps

Picture 62—Entire Front Pose

Picture 63—"Most Muscular" Pose

good balance between protein and carbohydrates, so include them all in your diet. And before going to the gym, you'll find that eating a few oranges will lend you welcome energy for harder training.

You may also wish to take some extra vitamins. I take vitamin C, for instance, just before I train; then again two or three hours after I finish training; then no more for the rest of the day.

SPORTSMANSHIP

This will probably come naturally to you. You and your fellow contestants have come together to compete in as fine a sport as I know. Without dignity, grace, and determination, you'd never have come this far. Only one of you will win. It's lots more fun to win than not to, but what are the absolutely worst consequences of losing? Simply not winning, as far as I can see. You've still got your same fine body and health, probably better than anyone you know. And there's always the next contest. So relax, give it your best, and be a good sport. You'll have more fun.

STAGE PRESENCE

I've said this before, too: Everybody was a beginner once. Rare indeed is the bodybuilder who wasn't nervous for his first contest.

But you can get over that. First, remember that the audience is on your side. Second, concentrate for a moment on all the fine bodybuilders you've leapfrogged past to get to the contest. Even before competition begins, you've achieved something that very few men could. Win, lose, or tie, I'd say you've earned a respectable dose of self-congratulations. You most certainly have mine.

On the other hand, don't go off on an ego trip either. You must communicate, with good judgment and taste, that you understand that despite your better body, you are no less human than your audience. Pose according to your personality, and what is most comfortable and best for you; and remember that a few good poses are far better than many poses which include a few clunkers. Bad poses will be remembered the same as good ones.

And more than anything else, good luck!

chapter sixteen

The title of my book is *Winning Bodybuilding,* but we don't mean by that that the idea is to build a better body than the next guy. Anyone who knuckles down, gets to work, and simply builds a better body is my idea of a real winner.

It's a wonderful sport. In many foreign countries, bodybuilding is one of the top two or three sports, and has been that way for years and years . . . even though their bodybuilders generally can't hold a candle to America's best! I can think of no other sport that rewards you so directly for what you bring to it, and that's as it should be. As I've said many times, in the beginning, it's just you and your body. Add someone else's knowledge and equipment, and you're off. And with a little determination and concentration, you can't miss.

My book should take you considerably less time to read than,

one last set

say, *War and Peace,* and yet the techniques between these covers are quite capable of leading you to the very top of the sport. But long before you get that far, if you ever do, you'll enjoy the singular thrill of seeing a body you like better than the one you had before.

That's a unique kind of joy. I know. I've been there. It's special because without any stages, or judges, you've competed against the body nature gave you, and won.

Some nice things have happened to bodybuilding in the last few years. We're finally getting the kind of visibility and publicity we want and need. Naturally, we want to keep that momentum. So once again, bodybuilding is like any other sport, in that we want fresh talent to help keep the ball rolling. Talent like you.

The very nature of the sport of bodybuilding is to make you

look good. Always try to do the same for the sport. And you and bodybuilding will continue to exchange benefits that way for many years.

Follow my book seriously and your maximum potential is well within your reach. I sincerely hope it helps make you a champion.

But whatever your goals, let's get to the gym and start winning.

index

standing press, 28, 29, 65-66
Side leg raises, 104-105
Side post, 129, 134
Sit-ups, 35, 39, 48, 101
Sleep, 113
Spinal column, 30
Sportsmanship, 146
Squat, 30, 32, 41, 83-86, 108
Stage presence, 146-147
Stages, of development, 24-26
Standing press, 28, 29, 65-66
Sugar, 118

T

Tan, sun, 129
Thighs
    leg curls, 42, 81-82
    leg extensions, 41, 81
    squat, 30, 32, 41, 83-86
Three-part wrist moves, 97
Training, 18-23, 135
    attitude, 110-113
Trapezius, 69
Triceps
    close-grip presses, 46, 48, 62-63, 92

extension: dumbbell, 95; lying, 46, 47, 90, 91
pushdowns, 92-93, 94
pushups, 35

U

Upright rowing, 69

V

Vacuuming, 100
Vitamins, 117, 146

W

Waist, 98-105
Warm-up, 120-122
    exercise, 28
Weaknesses, compensating for, 23
Weight, gaining, 117
Workouts
    frequency, 52-55
    time of day, 35
Wrist curls, 35, 37, 47, 97
    reverse, 47, 49, 97
Wrist moves, three-part, 97

BE SURE TO READ FRANCO COLUMBU'S OTHER GREAT BOOKS—AND DON'T FORGET THE FRANCO COLUMBU POSTER

23¼″ × 35″
COLOR